The HBCU Guide

The HBCU Guide

100+ Things to Know (and a Few Other Things You *Need* to Do)!

Robin M. May

iUniverse, Inc.
New York Lincoln Shanghai

The HBCU Guide
100+ Things to Know (and a Few Other Things You Need to Do)!

iUniverse books may be ordered through booksellers or by contacting:

iUniverse
2021 Pine Lake Road, Suite 100
Lincoln, NE 68512
www.iuniverse.com
1-800-Authors (1-800-288-4677)

ISBN-13: 978-0-595-35733-8 (pbk)
ISBN-13: 978-0-595-80210-4 (ebk)
ISBN-10: 0-595-35733-4 (pbk)
ISBN-10: 0-595-80210-9 (ebk)

Printed in the United States of America

To the 1993 freshman class of Clark Atlanta University: After Orientation Week, I knew that this was the school for me. Thanks for the many memories.

A special shout-out to:

- The ladies of Alpha Kappa Alpha Sorority Inc., Sweet Alpha Pi Chapter
- The Clark Atlanta Cheerleading Squad (1993–1995: Sexy Seven!)
- The Courts: B-6
- The Inspirational Voices of Faith (1993–1996)

Dedication

This book is dedicated to my cousin Ashley Williams. May you continue to strive for excellence in all you do. You are a star!

Acknowledgements

Much love and thanks to:

- God, who—like every rap-star, movie star and any other award-receiving person declares—is the head of my life. But no, honestly, it really is in Christ that I try to live, move and have my being. I pray that every book I author, every word I speak, and every life I touch somehow glorifies Him.
- My handsome husband, Lee Norris May, II— you are my covering, my lover, my life partner, my friend. I would have missed you even if we'd never met that first day on campus at CAU☺!
- My parents, Robert and Carolyn Simpson, and my sister Kimberly Alford—daily I am awed by your love for me, the sacrifices you've made and the support you give. It is my constant prayer that God returns more blessings to you than you can handle. You deserve it all.

Congratulations!

If you are considering attending a Historically Black College or University (HBCU), and you can't quite make up your mind; or, if you have already decided to attend an HBCU and your bags are packed; or even if you want to encourage someone you know to attend an HBCU because you had a blast during your experience, then you are definitely on the right track!

Dating as far back as 1837, the Historically Black College and University education is one that is held in the greatest esteem by its graduates. Those of us, who have walked across the stage, proudly holding our degree in hand, realize that we have not simply received an education, but we have acquired a unique experience that will never be duplicated. It is my hope that this fun guide to the HBCU life will be one to resonate strongly with you as you begin or continue your matriculation.

Throughout this guide you will occasionally see two asterisks (**). These represent tips that I believe are not only applicable to your college life, but also to your life in the "real" world. I call these tips, *Lessons For Life*. In addition, you will find one of the following at the end of each tip: *Check This Out (more information on that particular tip); Think On This (applicable quotes); Food For Thought (extended thoughts from me); Alumni Speak Out (testimonials from HBCU graduates); Did You Know (HBCU facts and other interesting information);* and, *Bragging Rights (famous alumni).* Also, at the end of the guide, you will find valuable resources for scholarships, suggested reading, etc. Applying these tips and seeking out the resources will help you be one of the most informed and prepared students on your campus! Finally, as you are reading these pointers, if you realize we've left something out, please feel free to send it to me…who knows, we may do a "HBCU Guide" Volume II! Regardless, we'd love to hear from you. E-mail us at info@hbcuguide.com or check out more information on the web at www.hbcuguide.com! In the meantime, keep learning, keep growing…always be open to change!

Contents

Student Life

1

Visit the campus of the school you are considering.

Never make a decision to live in an area for 4 years (and for some, 5 or 6 years if you don't heed these tips) without visiting it first. This one is pure common sense.

****

Check This Out

Many organizations sponsor college tours that allow potential students to check out the colleges of their choice. To find out more about tours in your area, search "college tours" on the Internet, ask your friends if they know of any tours, or speak to your guidance counselor.

2

Give the college experience time.

Shortly after enrolling in college, many students begin to think they've made a huge mistake. It's something like "buyer's remorse." Major life changes can be intimidating especially when you don't know what to expect. But I personally promise that, in most cases, if you decide to stick it out through your freshman year, you'll be glad you did. Things will turn out well in the end.

****

Think On This

"Consider the successes that resulted from tired, discouraged people who decided to give it just one more try."
—*Author Unknown*

3

Choose your friends carefully.

Just remember the ole' "birds of a feather" …saying! You may not be as wild as your hanging buddy, but you best believe that associations tend to lead to imitations.

****

Food For Thought

Although it is important to be careful of your associations, you shouldn't shun someone or be rude just because you don't agree with his or her actions. If one of your friends is living in a manner that is inconsistent with your values, take the time to share your concerns with the person. If you still feel uncomfortable with the relationship, gently let your friend know that although you need a little space, you still sincerely care about them.

4**

Meet new people.

I know, you're thinking, "duh," of course I'll meet new people. But this tip is to ensure that you are intentional about meeting new people. Introduce yourself; don't hang out with the same people you would normally hang out with. Go out of your way to be friendly. College relationships last a lifetime!

****

Lessons For Life

We often find ourselves drawn to people who are similar to us—people who feed our comfort zones. It is rare to find someone who intentionally seeks to be challenged by someone with a different opinion, philosophy or mindset. While in college and after graduating, make sure that you meet new people who are not like you. God made us uniquely different for a reason…find out why!

5

If you don't plan on getting involved or being social, don't go to an HBCU.

I may be biased, but I believe an education from an HBCU can match that of any other institution. However, one of the most important parts of the HBCU experience is in the camaraderie. If you are not into that, save yourself the money and go to a state school.

****

Alumni Speak Out

"As a second generation HBCU graduate, my parents instilled in me that the education, pride and friendships received as a result of attending a HBCU are priceless. I look back at my HBCU experience as the best time of my life! The pride it has instilled in me has helped me both in and outside of the office environment. I participated in an exchange program where I attended a mainstream college for one year. That experience reinforced for me why HBCUs are so special. The history, the knowledge and the drive to prepare you to be the best are incomparable."

Kia Jefferson
Lincoln University, Class of 1993
Public Relations Executive

6

Find out if your parents have friends in the city.

I know, I know—you are doing all you can to get away from your parents. Why would you want to hook up with someone that can be their eyes and ears? But this could really work to your advantage. Just think, you can wash your clothes for free, *and* you'll have home-cooked meals. It's worth it…well, sometimes.

****

Did You Know

The television show "A Different World" was set at a fictitious historically black college (Hillman College). Although not a real school, the show closely resembled the life of a student at a HBCU. In fact, many high school students chose to attend a black college or university based on the story line of this television show.

7

Don't get too excited about the cafeteria food during orientation week!

All I'll say to this is…*it changes*!

****

Check This Out

You know how it is when you or your parents are expecting company at the house? You always put forth your best foot to impress your guests. Well, this is what happens during orientation week at most schools. The administration knows that parents will be there so they put forth their best. But hey, can you blame them? Just know that this will be one of the things you will laugh about for years to come!

8

Learn the new definition of a three-course meal.

In college, a three-course meal consists of chips, dip, and a drink. You're really working it if you can get a dessert.

****

Bragging Rights

Toni Braxton, R&B singer and Grammy Award winner, attended Bowie State University. BSU is located in Bowie, Maryland and was established in 1865. The Bowie State University motto is: "Manly deeds, womanly words." Visit the school online at www.bowiestate.edu.

9

Public transportation—it *is* an option.

While in college, you will find a new appreciation in your heart for public transportation. Just make sure you are fully prepared for the show that will happen every day. I don't care what city you are in…some of the public transportation riders provide the best and cheapest entertainment you can find!

****

Check This Out

When you are riding public transportation in a new city, make sure you have someone with you at all times. This goes for males and females. Because you do not know the area, you may get lost the first few times you are out. It is better to find your way around with someone instead of trying to do it by yourself.

10

Become friends with someone who lives off campus.

Every so often you will definitely need a break from campus. Having a friend who lives off campus is a great plus. You'll feel like you are in a hotel, regardless if it's a run-down apartment!

****

Think On This

"A true friend laughs at your stories even when they're not so good, and sympathizes with your troubles even when they're not so bad."
                                        —Irish Proverb

11

Have fun!

This is another "duh" tip; however, you'd be surprised how many people actually go to college and think they are not supposed to have fun. That's ridiculous. Have a blast! Stay up late. Sleep in on the weekends. Dance like it's going out of style, and laugh until you cry! You may have heard it before, but it's true—the college years are some of the best times of your life.

****

Food For Thought

Have you ever heard older people reminiscing about a time in their life when things were really simple? This is that time for you! College is a time for you to really enjoy life and get to know yourself. Yes, it is crucial for you to apply yourself and take advantage of the education you have been afforded, but it is also a time for you to fully embrace all of college life. Try to have no regrets!

12

Take pictures.

Make sure that you take plenty of pictures of your friends, your roommates, your dorm, your teachers, the basketball games; football games...take plenty of pictures. You'll savor the memories.

****

Alumni Speak Out

When I started thinking about college, the only place I wanted to attend was Howard University in Washington, D.C. As a young, "negro" man growing up in a mostly segregated community in West Virginia, but attending newly integrated schools, Howard was it for me. All of my family had attended a majority college, but I wanted bigger. Howard and D.C. were terrifyingly big and complicated to my 17-year-old freshman self, but by my junior year I was flying high. There were no years like those years; I look back and treasure every moment.

Norman L. "Rocky" Jones
Howard University, Class of 1968
Family Therapist, Coach, Consultant

13

Keep your freshman T-shirt or hat.

Most freshmen are trying so hard not to be associated with *being a freshman*; however, you can forget it! It's obvious you are a freshman. The upperclassmen know it. So go ahead and wear your freshman T-shirt and hat…and keep it even after you graduate. Makes for more good memories.

****

Did You Know

Xavier University is one of the highest-ranking schools in the nation in placing African-American students into medical schools. Xavier is located in Louisiana and is uniquely America's only historically black and catholic university.

14

Take your yearbook picture.

When it comes time, make sure you take class pictures for your yearbook...*each year!* You'll want the memories 5, 10, 20 years down the line.

****

Bragging Rights

Walter "Sweetness" Payton, former pro football running back, attended Jackson State University. Jackson State was founded in 1877 and is located in Jackson, Mississippi. The school's motto is "You shall know the truth and the truth shall make you free." Visit JSU online at <u>www.jsums.edu</u>.

15

Carry a pencil and a pen at all times.

The pencil is for the temporary numbers in the phone book. The pen is for the permanent.

****

Alumni Speak Out

"My dad's military career kept my family living in ethnically diverse areas. When he retired in the south, blacks made up 51 percent of my high school, which is something I had never experienced. After getting to know others, I noticed that regardless of our economic or parental situations, there was a sense of comfort. I decided to attend a HBCU to further explore that sense of belonging. At Fisk University I felt at home. My professors not only knew me by my first name, they knew my family members by their first names. The support and love I received from Fisk University made me who I am today."

Allana W.
Fisk University, Class of 2001
Commercial Producer

16

Request a meeting with the President of your college.

Hey, it's worth a shot. Keep pursuing it each semester until you get the appointment. Once you do, just introduce yourself to him/her. Don't ask for anything, just let the President know who you are, your major, where you are from, and what your goals are after graduation. You never know how this small step may help you in the future.

****

Check This Out

Most students don't realize that they are employers! Students at colleges around the world employ the professors, administration and even the president of the school. This does not give the student a license to be disrespectful, but it does give the student the right to expect a certain standard from the people in leadership. Once you choose the college of your choice, remember to be involved in all aspects of the school.

17

On most HBCU campuses, if you're interested in a Greek organization, the goal is to be seen, not heard!

In other words, most organizations are not looking for the loudest, wildest, most "out there" man or woman to represent their group. Volunteer, get good grades, participate in campus activities. Allow who you are to speak louder than what you say.

****

Think On This

"No matter where you go, who you meet or what you do—make an impression. Master the unspoken word."
—*Author Unknown*

18

Be careful with sharing clothes.

Ladies, your girlfriends will quickly ask to borrow your bathing suit, jeans, shorts, etc. An unspoken rule: don't lend anything that goes between your legs. All I'm saying is, "Be careful!"

****

Bragging Rights

Lionel Richie, composer and songwriter, attended Tuskegee University. TU is located in Tuskegee, Alabama. The university was founded in 1881, and alumni, administration and students encourage you to "Come experience the spirit of Tuskegee." Find out more at www.tuskegee.edu.

19**

Don't lend it if you aren't willing to give it.

Go ahead and chalk this one up twice as a life rule. Whether it's a shirt, money or a book, if you aren't willing to part with it, don't lend it. This will help you keep a lot of potentially lost friendships.

****

Lessons For Life

When it comes to certain things in life, we often have to learn through experience. However, this is one lesson that you should take heed to without personally experiencing it: when you lend something to someone, only lend what you can do without! If you think along these lines, you will protect yourself from unnecessary stress. Most times, people tend to lose, break or forget to return what was borrowed.

20

Never date two men or two women in the same fraternity or sorority.

This will never work well in your favor. Chapter retreats kill the game every time!

****

Food For Thought

Okay, I know this seems like such a simple, playful tip, but it is so true. What is done in private always comes out, so if you are playing with fire, prepare to get burned.

21

Bring plenty of bug spray, powder and fly swatters.

Sorry, but they don't show you this part in the brochures!

****

Did You Know

According to the United Negro College Fund's HBCU facts, the majority of African-American public school teachers, African-American dentists and African-American physicians earned one of their degrees from a historically black college or university.

22

Do not park in yellow zones or no parking zones.

This is not downtown, any city, USA where you can park illegally all day and maybe get a ticket 1 out of 300 times. On many HBCU campuses, you *will* get ticketed, booted, or worse yet, *towed!*

****

Bragging Rights

Medgar Evers, Civil Rights activist, attended Alcorn State University. Founded in 1871, Alcorn State is located in Claiborne County, Mississippi. The school's colors are purple and gold. Visit Alcorn State online at www.alcorn.edu.

23

Study hard, and party just as much!

Every Bible-toting, Spirit-praying, church-going person is probably shaking a finger at this one. But I carry my Bible, pray in the Spirit, and go to church every Sunday—I still say: "Study hard, and party just as much!" This is college after all. Just make sure that it's clean, legal, safe, non-sinning fun. (I promise, there is such a thing!)

****

Alumni Speak Out

"I am fortunate to have a diverse background. Growing up, I lived in a predominantly white neighborhood and I commuted to an all black elementary and middle school. I attended my neighborhood high school, which was 90 percent Caucasian. At the end of my high school senior year, I chose to attend Prairie View A&M University. I received a presidential scholarship to attend PVAMU. My college years were awesome. I had teachers who were dedicated to my success, small interactive classroom settings and a chance to develop socially and academically. I became active in politics and learned more about myself and the rich history of black Americans, as Prairie View A&M was a prior slave plantation. The people I met in college are essential parts of my life today. I encourage all young students to consider attending a HBCU, as it was one of the best experiences of my life."

L. M. Edwards
Prairie View A&M University, Class of 2001
Insurance professional

24

Know your school's curfew policy.

There have been many freshmen who arrived on some HBCU campus thinking they were finally free! But *do know* that many of these schools impose a (much needed) curfew for freshmen.

****

Think On This

"Leadership consists not in degrees of technique but in traits of character; it requires moral rather than athletic or intellectual effort, and it imposes, on both leader and follower alike, the burdens of self-restraint."

—*L.H. Lapham*

25

Know your school's visitation policy.

Just like curfews, many dorms at HBCU's have visitation policies for the opposite sex. No fellas, she cannot spend the night. (But since she has this guide, and hopefully, if she pays attention to tip 36, she wouldn't be willing to anyway!)

****

Did You Know

The first Greek letter sorority founded by African-American women, Alpha Kappa Alpha Sorority Inc., was founded on a historically black college campus, Howard University. In 1908, Alpha Kappa Alpha was birthed to enhance the lives of college women in all aspects of life, particularly socially and intellectually. Having now grown to an international sisterhood with an emphasis on service, the ladies of Alpha Kappa Alpha are intimately involved in the black college experience.

26

Make friends with people who have cars.

No, I am not encouraging you to be a leech, or a user. But, it is good to have a friend who has a car—especially if your school is in a rural area. Make sure you give up the gas money though.

****

Think On This

"A true friend never gets in your way—unless you happen to be on your way down".
—*A. Glasow*

27

If you are interested in being a member of a particular Greek organization, join other organizations that are populated by those members.

By doing this, you gain an opportunity to meet the members of the particular organization you are interested in joining.

****

Bragging Rights

Dr. Martin Luther King Jr.—preacher, activist, Nobel Peace Prize recipient, and member of Alpha Phi Alpha Fraternity Inc.—attended Morehouse College in Atlanta, Georgia. Morehouse College for men is a part of the Atlanta University Center. The school's motto is "And There was Light." Visit Morehouse at www.morehouse.edu.

28

Attempt to build personal (*yet professional*) relationships with staff workers.

Why? First of all they are the engines behind the HBCU, and often times, can get things done for you much easier than you can do on your own. However, more importantly, they are usually great people who enjoy working with students and can prove to be a source of wisdom and knowledge during your matriculation.

****

Alumni Speak Out

"The moment I walked onto the campus of Hampton University I knew it was the place for me. The campus was amazing and had so much character. My eyes were opened to different cultures, music and style of dress of black people from all across the nation. It was an absolute honor to be in the midst of intelligent, young African-Americans with such bright futures. I am thoroughly convinced that without HU, I would not be where I am today, and I know the best is yet to come!"

Courtnee S.
Hampton University, Class of 2001
Account Executive

29

Invite your instructors to one or more of your organizational events.

This builds an inroad with them if you begin to miss class (like when it's warm outside). Do not take advantage of this relationship, but if your professor knows that you are involved in campus, they may be more lenient towards you. Again, this will only work if you do not take advantage of this tip *and* you are still on top of your assignments!

****

Food For Thought

One of the special qualities of historically black colleges and universities is the individualized attention professors give to students. As a student, it is advisable that you appreciate this aspect of your experience and include your professors in your extracurricular activities.

30**

Remember, a new car does not make you attractive!

This is such a life lesson it's not even funny! How many times have you met someone who thought he was so fine just because he drove a nice ride? Ladies, this goes for you too. Please! All it does is make you an *unattractive* person with a nice ride.

****

Lessons For Life

Unfortunately we live in a society that places extreme focus on what people have rather than who people are. This attitude motivates many people to place their personal worth in material possessions. As you continue to mature in life, remember to strive to be an attractive person because of your great character and integrity, not because of an overpriced ride!

31

Participate in homecoming activities.

Homecoming time can be the catalyst for some of your greatest memories, but it's all in what you make it. You'll regret it after you graduate if you don't participate.

****

Think On This

"When you dance, your purpose is not to get to a certain place on the floor. It's to enjoy each step along the way."

—*Wayne Dyer*

32

Run for office while in school.

No, no…not the Presidency of the United States. Let's bring it down a notch. Run for Student Government President, or run for an office in your favorite organization. This will show your leadership qualities and your ability to handle multiple responsibilities. After graduation, this will also set you apart in case your grades are equal to your competition.

****

Bragging Rights

Oprah Winfrey, talk show host and revolutionary media icon, attended Tennessee State University. Located in Nashville, TSU was founded in 1912. The university's motto is "Think, Work, Serve…It's What We Do." Learn more about Tennessee State at <u>*www.tnstate.edu*</u>*.*

33

Purchase each year's yearbook.

This is another one for your down-the-line memories. Can't you see yourself with lil' CeeCee saying, "That was me when I was a junior at one of the best HBCU's in the country!" Well if you can't, just know you'll be happy about it one day.

****

Alumni Speak Out

"My brother, a HBCU graduate, talked me into attending a historically black college. Initially I attended a majority college in the state of California and felt isolated, alone and as if the professors did not care. This may not be the experience of the other students, but it was definitely how I felt. My later experience at Philander Smith College was totally different. My professors were available, well prepared and connected with the community. I am encouraging my children to attend PSC or the HBCU of their choice. It really gives you a sense of pride and one less obstacle (racism, separatism and isolation due to your ethnicity) to deal with during your college years."

Cynthia M.
Philander Smith College, Class of 1989
Executive Director

34

Learn the value of the smell test!

I have to point this one more to the fellas…a few male friends told me that a guy's dirty clothes are all relative and must be put to a smell test before they go to the wash. I guess!

****

Bragging Rights

Historian, poet and Civil Rights activist W.E.B. DuBois attended Fisk University. Fisk is located in Nashville, Tennessee, and the school colors are gold and blue. Established in 1866, Fisk University can be found online at www.fisk.edu.

Taking Up Residence

35

Have your housing secured before your arrival.

Make sure that your housing is secure. Don't assume that you're all set just because you requested housing, sent in a deposit, and got a receipt. You need to have a dorm name, room number, and address before arriving on campus.

****

Did You Know

College bound students have a plethora of black colleges to choose from. There are more than 100 historically black colleges and universities in the United States. Although the majority of the schools are located in the southern and eastern regions, there are also HBCU's in Missouri,
Ohio and in the Virgin Islands.

36

Ladies, *stay out of the men's dorm!*

Yes, you are (almost) grown now, and you are away from your momma and daddy…but trust me on this one: your name and number will usually end up on someone's bathroom wall the next morning! I've seen it happen to many a "daddy's baby girl." Wouldn't daddy be too embarrassed if he happened to see your name on the wall (talk about shamed)?

****

Food For Thought

I know it may not seem fair but the reality is that a male can hang out at a female dorm and not have his reputation messed up. If a female is constantly hanging around a male dorm, eventually she will be viewed as one of the loose girls on campus. Now, you might say that you don't care what others think about you, but let's be honest—who really wants to be known as easy or fast? Besides, it may seem old fashion, but if a guy wants to see you, let him come to you.

37

Always wear flip-flops in the bathroom.

Who wouldn't? Gross! But just in case, no matter how comfortable you get, never go into the dorm bathrooms without your flip-flops. Trust me on this one. Your feet will thank you.

****

Did You Know

In 2002, Nick Cannon starred in a film titled "Drumline." The movie was based on the average marching band at a historically black college or university. At most HBCU's, the marching band is a very energetic and important part of the college experience. Clark Atlanta University's marching band (along with other college students) participated in the filming of "Drumline."

38

Never date two women that reside in the same dorm.

Bathroom talk kills the game every time!

****

Food For Thought

I know we talked about this earlier, but one more time won't hurt. Fellas, there are more women than men on most historically black college and university campuses. I know that this makes it very difficult to stay focused, but know that what you think you're doing on the low will get out! The game always catches up with you…it never fails.

39

Commit to campus housing for one full year at least once.

You need to experience dorm life in the fall and in the spring—two totally different experiences. After you've tried it, feel free to move into an apartment, but just remember that you have the rest of your life to be grown and pay bills each month. Some of us "grown folk" wish we could move back into a dorm…well, maybe not, but I think you get the point.

****

Bragging Rights

James Weldon Johnson, author and poet, attended Atlanta University (now Clark Atlanta University). Clark Atlanta University is located in Atlanta, Georgia and is a part of the Atlanta University Center family of schools. Established in 1988, Clark Atlanta's mottos are "I'll Find a Way or Make One" and "Culture for Service." Clark Atlanta University's website is www.cau.edu.

40

Have a heart-to-heart with your roommate.

Once you and your roommate settle in on the first day, have a heart-to-heart discussion. Set "house" rules. Do this regardless if the two of you are already friends. Put expectations on paper so that there are no surprises. For example, are you okay with her man being there *every* morning you wake up?

****

Check This Out

Once you have been accepted into school and you know the dormitory where you will reside, contact the dorm director. Some schools will even give you the contact information for your future roommate before the two of you arrive on campus. This way, you can start getting to know one another beforehand. Ladies particularly enjoy this information because it helps in coordinating your dorm room interior design!

Academic Experience

41

If you are a junior in high school, fill out your applications now and mail them on the last day of school during the same year.

This will allow you to be accepted early and have a head start on getting a full scholarship; then you won't have to be stressed about financial aid.

****

Think On This

"It's not the will to win that matters—everyone has that. It's the will to prepare to win that matters."
—Paul "Bear" Bryant

42**

Let high school go!

Please, pretty please, do not wear your sports jacket from high school. That is *too too* lame…please let it go! No one cares that you were the football star or cheerleading captain at XYZ Academy High School. Click your heels, Dorothy—you're not in Kansas anymore.

****

Lessons For Life

This tip is a life lesson that many adults haven't quite learned. The point in this tip is that seasons change and you are wise to change with them. You may have been the "man" or "woman" in sports or in school, but that season has come and gone. Make your mark where you are now. Let go of the past and Grab hold to where you are in the present.

43

Be intentional when developing your class schedule.

Build your schedule around when you are most productive. For instance, are you more alert first thing in the morning, mid afternoon, or sometime after 4 p.m.? Do your best to work around your greatest time of productivity.

****

Alumni Speak Out

"I do not regret attending a HBCU and would strongly recommend it to high school students that are in the process of selecting a college or university. I not only received a top-notch education, but I also am able to stay in close contact with many of my professors who continue to guide me in my choices pertaining to my own small business and career. I have only worked at the best firms since graduation; I owe much of my success to the education and hands-on training I received from my HBCU."

M. Reid
Bowie State University, Class of 1998
HR Generalist

44

When in doubt, pursue a liberal arts degree.

In our current economy, finding employment can be difficult. And it may be even more challenging when you are confined to a major that requires specialized training. Majoring in liberal arts (or other similar programs) gives you a greater range of options. However, I firmly believe that ultimately you should pursue your passion—so if you are motivated by engineering, mathematics or computer science, by all means stick to it!

****

Bragging Rights

Earl Vernon Monroe, former professional basketball player, attended Winston-Salem State University. Established in 1867, WSSU is located in Winston-Salem, North Carolina. The school motto is "Enter to Learn, Depart to Serve." Visit WSSU at www.wssu.edu.

45

Strongly consider a dual-degree program.

A dual degree gives you an opportunity to graduate with not only your undergraduate degree, but also a master's degree. Yes, you will be in school a year or two longer, but you will be way ahead of the game because of it!

****

Think On This

"Nothing limits achievement like small thinking, and nothing expands possibilities like unleashed thinking."
—*William Arthur Ward*

46

Choose three areas of interest.

When deciding what HBCU to attend, choose three areas that you would like to study, and then choose a school that has all three majors. This way you will have options once you actually get to school, just in case you haven't made up your mind on your major.

****

Check This Out

I often hear people say they don't know what they want to do in life. It may sound corny, but one of the greatest ways to find out your interests is to take interest inventories. Do a search on the Internet and you'll find hundreds of them. Choose one of the free tests, take it and see if it matches up with what you enjoy. Remember that you should always pursue your passion—profit will always follow you when you are doing what you love.

47

Remember why you are there.

Yes, have fun. Meet new people. Get involved. But don't forget that your primary reason for being there is to get an education from an esteemed institution.

****

Food For Thought

If I gave you a bag filled with money and told you to do whatever you wanted with it, would you take the bag outside, empty it and let the money fly away from you? I am sure you wouldn't, but why? Surely it is because you wouldn't want to senselessly waste the money. Take this same mindset with you when you enter college. School costs money! Even if you are on scholarship, you still will likely need to make some financial investment. Don't waste your time or your money. Stay focused.

48

Go to class.

Duh, yet again…but hey, I have to say it—*go to class*! While in some cases you *may* be able to skip class and not have anyone ever call or check up on you, a professor's discretion in grades can often reflect poor attendance, bad attitudes, or inappropriate behavior. So, in other words, in college, you're being graded on more than work and performance.

****

Think On This

"Intelligence plus character—that is the goal of true education."
—*Dr. Martin Luther King Jr.*

49

Start off strong.

Get good grades early, because there will be a time when your grades will "fall off"…like around homecoming, the first of spring, the first of winter….

****

Bragging Rights

Poet and playwright Langston Hughes attended Lincoln University in Chester County, Pennsylvania. The school was founded in 1854. Its motto is "If the Son shall make you free, ye shall be free indeed." Visit Lincoln University at www.lincoln.edu.

50

Study daily.

If you study daily, even if it's just a little bit, you won't have to cram for exams, and you won't end up forgetting all the material you memorized!

****

Alumni Speak Out

"My original plans were to attend a HBCU away from Nashville, Tennessee. However, I later decided not to leave Nashville, so I attended old reliable Tennessee State University. I look back fondly on my experiences at TSU. I still use the many skills that I learned in my courses there. I also enjoy the camaraderie among the TSU alumni. Since I've moved away from Nashville, I have been pleasantly surprised to meet many fellow alumni; we all enjoy reminiscing about our time at TSU."

Jackie J.
Tennessee State University, Class of '89
Senior Medical Underwriter

51

Participate in an internship program.

This will bring valuable experience and set you apart from many other applicants upon graduation. Even if you aren't sure exactly what you want to do after graduation, this will still look good on your resumé. Employers look to see that you have some work experience. Whether it is paid or not doesn't matter.

****

Check This Out

A great organization to research regarding internships is the Inroads program. (See the resource section of this book.) It is never too early to start looking for an internship. This is also a great way to make sure you are pursuing a field that is a good fit for you.

52
Study abroad.

Never again will you be in a position in which you can actually leave the country to study your favorite subject for an entire semester with no responsibilities back home. Even if you can't ever imagine traveling overseas, do it! Being exposed to different countries and/or cultures is invaluable personally and professionally. This one you'll never regret, even if for some reason you weren't fond of the country.

****

Did You Know

African-Americans have not always had access to higher education. Before 1964, blacks were usually excluded (with a few exceptions) from the privilege of attending a college or university. The beauty of the HBCU is that it has always been a place of refuge, opportunity and strength for African-Americans.

53

Get a written degree plan.

Once you've determined your major, get an appointment with your department chair. He/She will walk you through the rest of your entire matriculation on paper. Make sure that it is signed by the department chair, and then stick to it—unless of course you change your major.

****

Food For Thought

My favorite book in the world (and in my opinion, the most important one) teaches that without a vision you will perish. Even if you don't believe in the Bible, this scripture should still make sense to you. If you don't know what direction you are going in (in your case, graduation), or the steps (classes) it takes to get there, your efforts will be in vain.

54

Get a roommate who is majoring in the same thing you are, if possible.

By doing this, both of you will always have a partner accessible to help when the work gets a little tight.

****

Bragging Rights

Toni Morrison, world-renowned author and Nobel Prize recipient, attended Howard University. Located in Washington, D.C., HU was founded in 1867. Howard University's motto is "Truth and Service" and the school mascot is the Bison. Visit Howard University at <u>www.howard.edu</u>.

55

Always remember the dates for the last days to drop a class.

Yes, you can drop a class up to a certain time. No, you can't do it right before you take your finals, but you do have enough time to discover whether or not you can really handle the material. Remember, it's always better to drop the class than to fail the class. Just dust yourself off and try again.

****

Check This Out

In most cases your professor will be willing to work with you if you are having a difficult time in a class. Don't automatically choose to drop a class because it appears to be too difficult. Schedule an appointment with your professor to discuss what problems you are having before you decide to throw in the towel.

56

If you buy used books, make sure they are the *right* used books.

Before you buy a used book, please make sure that the book your teacher requires is not a *new* edition, which could include *new* chapters, deleted information, corrections and/or updates.

****

Alumni Speak Out

As a child I knew I wanted to attend college. When the time came for me to choose a school, I was afraid that attending a historically black college or university would be settling. Because I was a track star in high school, the sport was a major influence on where I attended school. I participated in many college tours and when I ran the pelican relays on Southern University's bright blue track, I fell hard for the university. Since graduating I am involved in so much, including being an activist; fitness enthusiast; recipient of numerous awards; a former pro-athlete; actress and producer of my own one-woman show; a model; and, Miss Black Georgia USA 2005. I wouldn't change my choice to attend a HBCU for anything in the world!

Claudia H. Anthony
Southern University, Class of 2001
Arts Professional

57

When necessary, get a tutor.

Tutors are great. Sometimes all you need is a little one-on-one instruction and guidance to take you to the next level. Now, if you know you have a problem with distraction, get a tutor that you are *not* attracted to!

****

Food For Thought

Students often hesitate to pursue additional assistance outside of the classroom setting. Quite frankly, that is foolish. If you need assistance, don't hesitate to ask for it. What often works well is to find someone who may be struggling in an area in which you are efficient. This way, the two of you can help one another. Remember, no man is an island unto himself.

58**

Learn to write and speak well.

Poor speech and writing will hamper even the most intelligent, capable professional. Consider taking a writing course, even if it isn't required. Think about getting involved in Toastmasters International for at least one semester. This investment in yourself will greatly pay off.

****

Lessons For Life

Let's get something clear—there is no such thing as "talking black" or "talking white." You should strive to talk properly, using correct grammar and a well-rounded vocabulary. If you know that this is an area for you that needs improvement, start working on it now. This is vitally important for your future success, both personally and professionally.

59**

Learn to speak another language, fluently.

Ebonics does *not* count! Having a foreign language skill will be useful in any field. In fact, at the very least, everyone should learn to speak Spanish since it's the most widely spoken language globally.

****

Lessons For Life

Many young people are motivated by the mighty dollar, so keep this tip in mind. Being able to speak another language fluently has the potential to almost double your salary in some professions. In addition, if you have aspirations for business ownership, being able to at least speak Spanish will increase your bottom line tremendously.

60

Find a mentor.

Seek out someone that you can learn the ropes from—someone who will look out for you. Make sure it's someone you respect. A good way to start is to find out about your hometown's alumni association for your school. For instance, if you attend or plan to attend Clark Atlanta University (*Go Panthers!*), and you live in Dallas, get connected with CAU's Dallas Alumni Association. You'll meet recent graduates who can hook you up with students still in school.

****

Bragging Rights

James L. Farmer, a leader in the Civil Rights Movement, attended Wiley College. Located in Marshall, Texas, Wiley College was established in 1873. The school's motto is "Achieving Excellence Through Pride and Performance." The Wiley College school colors are purple and gold, and the website is www.wileyc.edu.

61

Develop real study habits!

We're talking real study habits, not cramming skills. What good is it to retain information only to pass a test? This "just-enough-to-get-by" mentality will not help you succeed and reach your highest potential.

****

Think On This

"Education is more than a luxury;
it is a responsibility that society owes to itself."
—*Robin Cook*

62

Do your research on professors.

Ask older students about professors, instead of just blindly selecting or accepting any available instructor. However, don't always opt for the professor who has a reputation for being easy. You still want to be challenged in your education and pushed beyond what is comfortable.

****

Alumni Speak Out

Attending Spelman College was so right for me that I think I was born for it! During my matriculation I was surrounded by intelligent, attractive and thoughtful women who, on top of all of that, still knew how to party hard and have a good time. In high school I was always one of the most talented, intelligent and fun students. It was an adjustment to be surrounded by all of these men and women (in the Atlanta University Center) who had everything I had going for me and even more. My experiences at Spelman, the ones that made me cry and the ones that bought me joy, helped form me into the woman I am today. There is absolutely nothing like a HBCU.

Amila T. Jones
Spelman College, Class of 1997
Spanish Teacher

63

Obtain past tests from students who have previously taken your current professors' classes.

I am *not* encouraging you to cheat. However, if you know someone has taken a class from a particular professor already, ask to see the professor's test. At least you'll know what to expect.

****

Did You Know

Statistics have shown that black colleges and universities award one out of every six master's degrees or first-time professional degrees earned by African-Americans. Research has also shown that many of the black college students that go on to receive advanced degrees (whether at a majority university or a HBCU), received their undergraduate degree from a black college.

64

Stay in contact with your professors.

Make sure you keep in contact with your professors once you finish with your classes. Well, make that *the professors that taught the classes you excelled in.* Do this even while you are still in school, and also after you leave. You may need them for recommendations.

****

Check This Out

This tip is critically important and is one that was part of the catalyst for this book project. When I decided to pursue an advanced degree, I had trouble finding a professor that could give me a recommendation. Keep in mind that I graduated with honors from Clark Atlanta University, however I did not keep in touch with my professors. Even if you end up in a totally different field than what you have studied, companies and graduate schools want to know how you were able to handle your academic responsibilities. So, while in school and even after you graduate, send professors an email every once in awhile keeping them abreast of what is going on in your life.

65

Don't allow anyone to belittle your pursuit of education.

Let's face it—everyone in your life may not be excited that you are attempting to make a better way for yourself. Someone will attempt to convince you that you don't need college…that you can do just like him/her and stay in your hometown and hustle. Shake the haters off and keep going!

****

Bragging Rights

Shannon Sharpe, former football player with the Denver Broncos, attended Savannah State University. SSU is located in Savannah, Georgia and was established in 1890. Savannah State's mascot is the tiger and their colors are blue and orange. The school website is <u>www.savstate.edu</u>.

Personal Growth

66

Try to go to an out-of-state school.

Of course, Granny wants you to stay in Rayville. But if at all possible, try to go to school out of state or at least two or three hours from your hometown. One of the benefits of college is that it teaches you to fend for yourself, and it also teaches you to mature—before you are *really* out there by yourself. How can you mature with your momma and 'nem still doing everything for you?

****

Food For Thought

This tip is often difficult for parents to accept. However, it is vital that parents allow college to be more than an educational experience. It is also a great life experience, particularly if the student is away from his or her home state. As a student, venture out...move away...try someplace new.
You won't regret it.

67**

Pray!

Yes, pray. Pray in the morning, pray at night, pray during the day, pray before the test, pray during the test, pray after the test, pray at the club, pray at the house party, pray in the cafeteria (please pray in the cafeteria), pray walking to class…whatever you do, *pray*! It will sustain you.

****

Lessons For Life

I know, I know, this is not Sunday school, but hear me out. To use a phrase from one of my mentors… "in my humble but accurate opinion," there is no hope without prayer. God created you, and so of course He longs to talk with you. We make time for everything else in our lives. Make it a point to spend some uninterrupted time in prayer. If you don't think you know how to pray, find someone who does who can help you. People always say that prayer changes things. I like to say that prayer changes you and positions you to know, accept and submit to the will of God. Okay, enough…church is dismissed.

68**

Trust your gut.

If something feels wrong, then it is. Have the courage to say so and tell someone in authority.

****

Lessons For Life

Have you ever finished taking a test, decided to go back and change one answer, and afterwards found out that your first answer was right? What was your first reaction? Most times you think, "I should have gone with my first mind." This is so true in life. In most cases, when it doesn't feel right, it's not right. Trust your instincts. If you feel like a situation is dangerous or could potentially lead to a negative end, remove yourself. Although college campuses take great precaution to keep students safe, no place is fail proof. Most of the responsibility for your safety falls on your own shoulders. Be aware and be careful.

69

"Freestyle" for your first year, if necessary.

Most people at 18 (or 30 for that matter) are not ready to make up their minds about what they plan to do for the rest of their lives. Freestyle during the first year and find what you like; or just stay in the Registrar's Office while you change your major again, and again, and again. Your choice.

****

Alumni Speak Out

Being a tri-athlete in High school, I had thoughts and dreams of playing football for a large division 1 college. However, my decision was made after visiting Johnson C. Smith University and realizing that they would give me the opportunity to play two of the sports I loved...and a scholarship! I wouldn't trade my experience there for anything. The individual attention I received from both teachers and administrative staff was incredible. The best thing was that I wasn't just another number; I was an important part of the university family. The bonds I developed there are unforgettable and I believe that my educational development truly prepared me for my career.

Andrew L. Momon Jr.
Johnson C. Smith University, Class of 2002
Fitness Center Director

70

Don't be afraid.

These experiences will prepare you for the world. Every experience is a learning one. If it doesn't kill you, and it isn't illegal or immoral, it can only make you stronger. You are well able to do what you have set out to do. I dare you to believe in yourself and not allow fear (False Evidence that Appears to be Real) to stop you!

****

Bragging Rights

Andrew Young, U.S. ambassador and a former mayor of Atlanta, Georgia, attended Dillard University. Dillard is located in New Orleans, Louisiana and was founded in 1869. Visit Dillard University online at www.dillard.edu.

71

Remember your home training.

Now that you are in college, don't forget your manners! If your momma didn't let you do it at home, don't do it now. And if you didn't have any home training, get some.

****

Did You Know

Alpha Phi Alpha Fraternity Inc, the first intercollegiate Greek-letter fraternity for African-Americans, celebrated its 100th anniversary in 2006. Founded by seven men of distinction in 1906, Alpha Phi Alpha stands strongly on its history of being on the frontlines of many educational, political and social issues for African-Americans.

72

What you are to be, you are now becoming.

I know you've heard this pearl of wisdom before. Stop thinking you have forever to get it together, to become responsible, to show character, etc. Your actions today are shaping the person you are today and will be tomorrow. Bishop Eddie L. Long, pastor of New Birth Missionary Baptist Church in Lithonia, Ga., often asks his congregants a question that was posed to him: "If you die today, will it ever matter that you lived?" Make your life matter!

****

Think On This

"Far better it is to dare mighty things, to win glorious triumphs, even though checkered by failure, than to take rank with those poor spirits who neither enjoy much nor suffer much, because they live in the gray twilight that knows not victory nor defeat."
—T. Roosevelt

73

Find a church home.

It will keep you centered. There's even more of a plus to this: many of them will provide transportation to and from worship services, and a nice Sunday meal too!

****

Food For Thought

A startling statistic states that seven out of 10 students who attended church in high school no longer attend once they enter college. You will have many people, things and situations pulling at you while you're in school. Finding a church home will give you the security that you need as well as a much-needed source of accountability. A great way to find a church home is to ask your current pastor or church leadership for any suggestions on churches in your school's area.

74

Take a personality or gifts test.

So, you don't quite know what you want to be when you grow up! No problem. This is a perfect season in your life to find out. Take a personality and/or gifts test to find out what your strengths are to assist you with selecting a major.

****

Check This Out

This tip is similar to the explanation of tip number 46. However, there is a slight difference between determining your personality and determining your interests. These two can work together to assist you in pursuing your God-given passion.

75**

Take notes of important phone calls and meetings, especially when the subject is grades or money.

Because some teachers catch a case of amnesia, it helps if a college student has made specific notes about conversations: who participated, what date and time, about what, and the final outcome. Keep a folder dedicated to these types of conversations. It could save you one day.

****

Lessons For Life

This tip is particularly important in your post-college life. In dealing with your finances, meetings with your supervisor, or conversations with your future employees, it is vital to keep accurate records. This will ensure that there is no confusion when tough decisions have to be made or when it is time to correct any discrepancies.

76**

Copy, copy and copy again!

Here's another one that can save you. Keep a copy of *all* records, receipts, papers, grades…anything that can be copied, *copy it*! Just when you least expect, you will need to show proof.

****

Lessons For Life

Of course the Enron executives might disagree with this tip, but trust me, this is important in your post-college life. Make sure that you keep your copies in a fireproof safe or file cabinet. Also, after you graduate, make sure you also keep official and unofficial copies of your transcript.

77**

No matter how frustrating things may become, keep a pleasant attitude and remain professional.

People are more willing to help if you have a pleasant attitude in the time of trouble. A composed demeanor can be your ticket to "secret grants" if your money is ever at $0!

****

Lessons For Life

I didn't want to go there with an overly played quote, but here goes: "You always catch more bees with honey." Okay, I said it and it's true! No matter what the situation, the only person you can control is you. Keep your attitude in check and watch how situations tend to turn in your favor.

78**

Journal.

This one may sound a little corny, but do it. Keep a college life journal (you may need one for each year), and jot down special memories, tough times, exciting times, etc. You'll enjoy reading it when you are older.

****

Lessons For Life

I might be biased, but I truly believe that anyone reading this guide has an amazing future ahead of him or her. (I mean come on…you were smart enough to read this book!) This means that you will be doing big things, making history and changing lives. If you don't write your story along the way, there will be many people who will miss out on the valuable experiences and lessons you learn. Journaling is not just for you; it's for those coming after you. Start writing your life story now…I can't wait to read it.

79**

Observe the motives of others.

Unfortunately, not everyone is there to study or to get an education. Once you realize that, you can steer clear of troublemakers. Don't mess up a good opportunity while you have it.

****

Lessons For Life

I once heard my best friend Oprah say, (okay, so she may not know that she's my best friend, but once I can get Gayle out of the way...)"When someone shows you who they are, believe them." Reread that statement. People show us daily who they are and for some reason we don't believe them. Be quiet and watch the people around you. There is a purpose for your life and if there is anyone taking you off the path to that purpose, he or she should no longer be welcomed in your world.

80**

Be aware of the global world.

It's so easy to get caught up in campus happenings, but smart folks remember that they live in a larger community. Stay on top of news events. Read the paper and look at the news. It will make a big difference in how you view the world and will be good fodder for conversations with potential employers and social contacts.

****

Lessons For Life

Being aware of what is going on in your neighborhood, city and state is important but still very small-minded. It is important for us to realize that we should be concerned with issues all over the world. It may not affect us intimately or personally but because we are a part of the human race, we must turn our attention to the world as a whole.

81**

Never give up.

Someone on campus is always there to help, listen, and lean on.

****

Lessons For Life

In my life as I have pursued different goals, I've often felt like I could not go on and was ready to give up. But every time, the break that I needed came through. I have heard this same testament from very successful and well-known people who have reached a great level of success. Keep in mind that it is important to reevaluate your situation and make changes when necessary. But do not give up in life because things get too hard or there are too many obstacles. Fight harder, climb over the roadblocks, be a trailblazer. It isn't easy, but it surely is worth it.

82**

Give back…volunteer in the community.

Don't forget where you've come from. Even if your family is wealthy, your *people* have struggled. Give back every chance you get!

****

Lessons For Life

Have you ever heard someone say, "To whom much is given, much is required"? We often think that this is referencing money, but that isn't the only understanding of this thought. The fact that you are even in school means that you have something to give. It's weird, but in life, when you give you get. Mentor someone. Volunteer for an organization that you believe in. Do something to give back. You will find that the feelings you experience are more fulfilling than anything you could have ever expected to receive.

83

If you find God in school, stay with Him full-time.

Many times students truly understand God for themselves (not just because momma and daddy made you go to church) while in school. If you do, don't ever let Him go!

****

Food For thought

In today's culture, God is often placed on the back burner and only moved into a place of importance during crisis. This is unfortunate because God desires to be at the center (front, side and back for that matter) of our lives. Just like you have to spend time with someone to show him or her your love, God desires for us to spend time with Him and express to Him how crucial He is to our existence. If you have accepted God into your life, don't let it be a part-time pursuit.

84

Visit the homes of your friends during at least one of the holidays each year.

Many times it's an inexpensive trip; and you'll get a new experience.

****

Did You Know

Although there is a level of healthy competition amongst the African-American fraternities and sororities, greater than that is the true sense of unity. The National Pan-Hellenic Council Inc. is the unifying body for nine International Greek letter sororities and fraternities. The organizations represented in the NPHC are Alpha Phi Alpha, Fraternity Inc., Alpha Kappa Alpha Sorority Inc., Delta Sigma Theta Sorority Inc., Zeta Phi Beta Sorority Inc., Iota Phi Theta Fraternity Inc., Kappa Alpha Psi Fraternity Inc., Sigma Gamma Rho Sorority Inc., Phi Beta Sigma Fraternity Inc. and Omega Psi Phi Fraternity Inc.

85

Don't take yourself too seriously.

Just because you were the most popular, the smartest, the most beautiful, the most handsome, or the most athletic in high school, it means nothing now. You are starting from scratch, so allow me to break it to you as gently as possible: there will always be someone smarter, more attractive, and more athletic than you. Hard to believe, huh?

****

Bragging Rights

Jerry Rice, former NFL player, attended Mississippi Valley State University. MVSU is located in Itta Bena, Mississippi. Known as the Delta Devils, MVSU was founded in 1950 and its motto is "Live for Service." Visit Mississippi Valley State University on the web at www.mvsu.edu.

86

Develop good time management skills.

Without good time management skills, a project on which you are capable of getting an "A" may end up being a project on which you receive a "B" or a "C" instead. Also, if you are serious about your studies, you will have to skip some of those events that you *really* want to attend. Master your time.

****

Food For Thought

Time management can be described more accurately as setting priorities. In life when you find yourself maxed out or overwhelmed, the first step is to see how you are managing your priorities. A person of maturity is able to look at life as a whole to make sure he or she is on the right track. Once you determine your priorities, your time management will be more productive.

87**

Know yourself.

You have to know yourself and be secure in your own identity. When you arrive on campus, there will be so many things to identify with. But you have to make sure that the things you choose are a true representation of who you are deep down inside.

****

Lessons For Life

You are amazing. Yes, you. No matter how much you have gone through or what you've done wrong in your life, you are amazing. You have to believe that you are special and that you have so much to offer. However, to fully understand how "great" you are, you have to take the time to determine "who" you are! College is the best time to figure out your life. Take advantage of this opportunity.

88

Open the Bible at least once a day…and read it!

Yes, I know that everyone reading this hilariously funny and informative guide may not be a Christian. But hey, has a little wisdom ever hurt anybody? At least read Proverbs. (It's easy to find…it's in the middle of the Good Book!)

****

Food For Thought

If your car stopped running would you take it to a TV manufacturer to get it fixed? What if you couldn't figure out how to work your iPod? Would you read the manual that came with your Game Boy? It wouldn't make sense. Well, in order to find out what is in store for you, how to make the best decisions, or how to live in this life, consider reading the manual that gives us the Word from our Creator. Now that makes sense!

89

Travel.

During Thanksgiving breaks, Christmas breaks, Spring breaks, travel! Getting involved with extracurricular activities will present you with opportunities to travel. Experiencing new places helps you grow.

****

Alumni Speak Out

Attending and graduating from Texas Southern University was one of the best decisions and most memorable times of my life. Although mainly African-Americans attend HBCU's, there is still diversity in the backgrounds and experiences of the student body. HBCU's also have a smaller enrollment than the majority public institutions. This increases the opportunity for interaction with faculty rather than being known as a statistic or just a number. Smaller classes do not mean easier work; it means more attention. I have made lifelong relationships and I was prepared for the real world.

James W.
Texas Southern University, Class of 1998
Project Manager

90

Eat right. Exercise.

These are difficult ones, but do your best. Please believe that the "freshman 15" is not a myth…neither is the "Sophomore 20" nor the "Senior 40." Let's not talk about what happens once you graduate.

****

Bragging Rights

Ed Bradley, a prominent television journalist, attended Cheyney State College. Now known as Cheyney University of Pennsylvania, the school was founded in 1837. Known as the Wolves, CU can be found on the web at www.cheyney.edu.

91

Be willing to change your perspective.

For instance, a-$150 in your checking account really isn't *that* bad. Ramen noodles for dinner *really are* quite nice. Getting an hour worth of sleep *is* refreshing. It's all in your perspective.

****

Check This Out

Sometimes students get home sick as they start to experience the difficult times that come with being a college student on any campus. Again, change your perspective. Be willing to see things from a different point of view. It may not be easy at times, but your character will be strengthened as you stay in the game and eventually win.

92**

Learn how to make wise choices.

Sometimes you have to choose between buying a new 'fit or buying that biology book. Please make the right decision.

****

Lessons For Life

Choosing to buy a biology book over a new outfit speaks highly of your ability to make adult decisions. In your post-college life, help yourself make wise choices by associating with people whose lives reflect what you are trying to achieve. As you observe them, be intentional about learning how and why they do what they do. Begin applying what you learn to your own life and you will soon be on the right track toward excellence.

93

Enjoy the roller coaster of self-discovery.

You will find out more about yourself over the course of four years than you will about your major. Enjoy it!

****

Alumni Speak Out

After growing up in a predominantly white neighborhood, I had no doubt I wanted to be surrounded by other African-Americans when I went to college. I chose to go to Florida A&M University because of its amazing business program. While I attended FAMU, the college was selected as Time magazine's college of the year! Based on the professional development training I received at FAMU, I have been able to excel in the workforce and in one of the top law schools in the nation. Now I am employed at a successful law firm and working to open my own law practice. I wouldn't trade my experience at FAMU for anything.

Leigh K. Hughes, Esq.
Florida A&M University, Class of 1998
Business; Law

94

Dream big!

You name it; you can do it! There is absolutely nothing out of your reach. Step out there and challenge yourself…believe in yourself…this is the best time of your life.

****

Think On This

"To the degree we're not living our dreams, our comfort zone has more control of us than we have over ourselves."

—*Peter McWilliams*

95**

Reputations last.

However you present yourself the first year of college will likely carry you through the rest of your matriculation. How do you want to be remembered?

****

Lessons For Life

It's a fact that first impressions do make lasting impressions. Although we should not live our lives based on what others think about us, there is a direct relationship between how people think about you and how you are treated. We all want to be respected and we want our opinions to count. Therefore, in life, we have to be conscious of our actions and attitudes toward others.

Money Sense

96**

Do not get sucked into the credit card promotions.

You only need *one* credit card, and that is *only* if you have proven yourself disciplined enough to handle it. If you *do* get a credit card, make sure the limit is no more than $500. This card should be used only when *absolutely necessary*—do not use it to buy dinner, rent cars, or any other nonsense items. And only charge what you can pay off when the bill is due for the month.

****

Lessons For Life

Our nation is consumed by debt. Debt can be crippling and devaluing, and it can be the cause of emotional stress. There is a difference between good and bad debt. Do your research and learn the difference. However, I can save you some time. Credit cards are mostly considered bad debt. Do yourself a favor and stay away—far away—from this consuming habit. Give yourself a chance to live a life that is debt free. It is very freeing, and it is possible…even in our day and time.

97

Student loans—only borrow what is needed.

If you must use student loans, only accept what is needed to cover your room and board (i.e., you may qualify for a $7,000 loan, and you only need $5,000). Only request and accept what you need, and no more.

****

Bragging Rights

Presidential nominee, Civil Rights activist and preacher Jesse Jackson attended North Carolina Agricultural and Technical State University. North Carolina A&T was founded in 1891 and the school motto is "Mind and Hands." North Carolina A&T is located in Greensboro, North Carolina; the school's website is www.ncat.edu.

98

Make friends in the financial aid and scholarship office.

Many times the financial aid officers receive monies that they have to allocate quickly. They are more apt to contact people they know when these opportunities arise. As you are building relationships in this office, make sure that you are sincere. Also, don't just get to know the financial aid officer—get to know the receptionist, the secretaries, and the work-study students. They all could easily become a valuable resource to you.

****

Did You Know

Research has shown that historically black colleges and universities produce 40 percent of all African-American doctorates in the area of communications.

99

Apply for all scholarships.

Once there was a young man in the financial aid office. He was giggling out of control. When asked what was so funny, he said, "I applied for every scholarship and I qualified for them all. They are paying me to go to school…" after which he burst out laughing. *Apply for those scholarships!*

****

Check This Out

In Georgia, there was a young high school student who applied for so many scholarships that she was awarded more than $400,000 for school. Let me repeat that—$400,000! You may not be as fortunate as this young lady, but not having the money to go to school is no excuse. Applying for scholarships should be like a part-time job for you. Don't stop once you are accepted at the school of your choice. Continue to apply throughout your matriculation. Set a certain time of day that you will search for the money you need for school and fill out applications. Why pay for school when someone else wants to help you pay for it?

100**

Run from anything that promises easy money.

Do not fall for the "it's an easy way to make money" game. Do not agree to do anything illegal or immoral for money…it is not worth it. Listen to your *parents*. They do know a little something.

****

Lessons For Life

Nothing, again I say, nothing in life is free. There are many multilevel marketing scams, fake real estate opportunities and other easy money gimmicks that look so real and so appealing. However, life teaches that you should be leery if something comes without much effort on your part. Besides, what is so amazing about hard work is that when you achieve your goal, the satisfaction is worth all of the sweat and tears.

101

Learn to live within your means while in school.

If I could get on my knees and beg you to learn this tip, I would! I promise, if you do this one, it'll make your life so much easier. I never could understand how some of my classmates were rocking *all* of the latest gear until later I realized they were up to their eyeballs in credit-card debt once they got out of school. Don't try to be like the Joneses (the Smiths, the Jacksons or anyone else). I bet if you ask them, they'll tell you that they are broke!

****

Alumni Speak Out

Realizing the odds against me, I took full advantage of opportunities to grow socially and professionally on the campus of Morris Brown College. Attending a HBCU was a phenomenal experience. It was filled with life-changing opportunities that prepared me as a young African-American male. The continued support of the faculty and staff contributed greatly to my successful matriculation through college and, subsequently, life. Currently pursuing a doctorate, I recognize the benefits of having a strong undergraduate experience. Therefore, I encourage high school students to attend a historically black college.

Rasheen G. Booker, Ed.S.
Morris Brown College, Class of 2000
Education Administration

102

You *do* have to pay your student loans back.

Those hefty loans do catch up with you. It is *not* free money. Do whatever you can to get scholarships, and when you can't, then prepare for the big payback.

****

Check This Out

I know this tip sounds repetitive, but I have to make sure you get it. I met a young male college student that told me he didn't realize he had to pay back his student loans because he thought they were grants. Also, while I was in school, so many of my friends were always shopping and eating out and I couldn't understand why. Now I know they were using their loan money to fund an excessive lifestyle. Don't fall into this trap. Use only what you need—it is not free money.

On the Career Path

103**

Write out your life vision/mission statement and post it up where you'll see it often.

If you don't know where you're headed, how will you get there? Your vision may change, and if it does, rewrite it. But you must have a map for your destination.

****

Lessons For Life

Would you know how to get to my home if I didn't give you my address? How successful would you be if I gave you a box of materials without any directions and told you to build an object you've never seen? The point is this: without a mission, as well as an understanding of how to reach it, your efforts will be unproductive.

104

Purchase at least one dry-clean-only business suit for your interviews.

No, it's not okay to go to an interview wearing your favorite jeans and a nice jacket. Please be properly prepared.

****

Did You Know

In 2006, Spelman College celebrated 125 years of educating and empowering women. Founded in 1881, Spelman College is a women's college located in Atlanta, Georgia. The institution is proud to be one of the oldest black colleges for women in the nation.

105**

Use the career placement center (CPC).

The services that the CPC offers are free (well sort of…somewhere in the "miscellaneous fees" part of your tuition, they are getting theirs), so utilize them. Remember, it's easier to find a job while you are still in school.

****

Lessons For Life

Career counseling is a great tool for you to use even after you graduate from college—it will help keep you on the right track toward your ultimate career goals. Also, consider hiring a headhunter to help you search for a job. Take advantage of the relationships you built while in school. The networking that comes from the black college experience is extremely helpful to most graduates who know how to put it to work.

106

Consider volunteering for a potential employer.

A lot of companies offer internships. But if the field you want to enter doesn't have many internship opportunities, consider volunteering. By doing so, you will enjoy flexibility that you wouldn't have if it were a paid internship, and you'll still gain valuable experience.

****

Bragging Rights

Booker T. Washington, educator and author and the first principal of what eventually became Tuskegee University, attended Hampton University. Hampton is located in Hampton, Virginia and was founded in 1868. The school mascot is the pirate and the motto is "The Standard of Excellence, An Education for Life." Learn more about HU by visiting <u>*www.hamptonu.edu.*</u>

107

Apply to grad school early.

If you know you want to attend graduate school, start working on your applications early. Remember how successful the early bird was.

****

Did You Know

In 1988, the film "School Daze," written and directed by HBCU alum Spike Lee, debuted. The movie focused on the life of fraternities and sororities at a fictitious black college. Like "A Different World," "School Daze" was a very real depiction of black colleges. Most of the settings for the movie were filmed in the Atlanta University Center.

Whew! We're finally done. There you have it…your "HBCU Guide: 100+ Things to Know (and a Few Other Things You *Need* to Do!)"

I truly hope that I was able to put a smile on your face, while at the same time, give you some valuable tips. As mentioned before, the HBCU education is one to cherish. I wish you much success. God bless!

Resources

Note: This is *not* an exhaustive list of the many resources available to the current or college-bound student. Use these resources, but continue to research as much information as you possibly can.

✓ Program: INROADS (www.INROADS.org)
✓ Program: Monster Diversity Leadership (www.monsterdlp.com)
✓ Book: *Guaranteed 4.0*, by Johnson and Chen (www.nomorestudy.com)
✓ Book: *The 7 Habits of Highly Effective Teens*, by Stephen Covey (www.Franklincovey.com)
✓ Website: www.hbcuconnect.com (Provides resources for all aspects of the HBCU experience)
✓ Website: www.hbcunetwork.com (Provides networking with other HBCU students and alums.)
✓ Website: www.Vault.com (Career guide for college students)
✓ Website: www.wetfeet.com (Career Information by industry)

✓ Website: www.internshipPrograms.com
(Information on internships)

✓ Website www.assessment.com
(Free online career assessment)

✓ Website: www.mindsightinc.com
(Provides a high school to college academic transition tool.)

✓ Website: www.smart.net/~pope/hbcu/hbculist.htm
(A listing of HBCU websites)

✓ Website:
http://www.littleafrica.com/resources/colleges.htm
(A listing of HBCU mailing addresses, as well as names and titles of the school presidents)

✓ Website : www.nafeo.com (A portal of internships, conferences, job openings and more)

✓ Website: www.wetfeet.com
(Corporate recruitment solutions)

Additional Acknowledgements and Thanks:

- My Pastor and First Lady, Bishop Eddie L. Long and Elder Vanessa Long—thank you for awakening in me the power, strength and ability to believe God. The time is now...let's do this!
- The rest of my family, including my In-loves (we marry by love, not by law)—thanks for your love, prayers and your belief in my God-given gifts.
- Barton Taylor, Zenobia Story, and Amila Jones—thank you for your honest, yet loving critique/edit of this project.
- Lisa Birch of Harriston Birch Communications for your editing assistance. Your ability to encourage and critique is amazing.
- My extended family and friends, I am so blessed to have each of you. If I began listing names, I wouldn't be able to stop—so I won't start! However, you know who you are...and if you don't, well then, I don't know what to tell ya!

Special thanks go to the following people for their contributions...Lee May, Marla Young, Laura Pinkney, Nataki Eggleston, Kim Echols, Janis Moore, Andito Johnson, Daagye H. Harvill, Albert Brownlee, Sherri Phillips, Caniela Jarrell, LaKecia May, Bart Taylor, Sonique Sailsman, Lisa Bolden, Erik Burton, Traci Hobbs, April McLaughlin, Zenobia Story, Aqualyn Jones and Nanyamka Fisher.

978-0-595-35733-8
0-595-35733-4

LaVergne, TN USA
07 April 2010
178514LV00001B/87/A

9 780595 357338